M. E Robbins

Supplementary Lessons to Munson's Complete phonographer

M. E Robbins

Supplementary Lessons to Munson's Complete phonographer

ISBN/EAN: 9783337399818

Printed in Europe, USA, Canada, Australia, Japan

Cover: Foto ©Paul-Georg Meister /pixelio.de

More available books at **www.hansebooks.com**

SUPPLEMENTARY LESSONS

—TO—

Munson's Complete Phonographer.

CONTAINING

WORDS AND PHRASES FROM BUSINESS CORRESPONDENCE, CLASSIFIED UNDER CONDENSED RULES; ALSO, LISTS OF WORDS DISTINGUISHED, LAW TERMS, AND WORD-SIGNS AND ABBREVIATIONS, WITH THEIR PHONOGRAPHIC OUTLINES.

PREPARED BY

M. E. ROBBINS,

Cooper Union, New York.

NEW YORK.
1891.

LESSONS I., II., III.

25 CONSONANT STEMS.

Sounded as *p* in Pay, pill, put, pile, puff, pop, pool, peal, paw.
" " *b* " Bar, bake, but. big, beg, ball, bow, boom, book.
" " *t* " Tar, time, tea, tap, tell, took, tug, top, tool, toe.
" " *d* " Dark, day, deep, deck. dig, dawn, did, do, dock, dine.
" " *ch* " Charm, chain, cheek, check, chill, chalk, choke, chum, chop, cheer.
" " *j* " Jest, jar. jail, jeer, jam, jaw, joke, jump, June, joy.
" " *k* " Keep, kill, keg, keen, kick, key, kite, keel, kid, kind.
" " *g* " Good, gun, grown, gale, girl, grape, guide, give, game, guess.
" " *f* " Far, fame, feel, fair, fed, fill, foe. fool, fun, foot.
" " *v* " Veil, veal, van, very, vim, vault, vote, vied, void, vow.
" " *th* " Theme, thank, theft, think, thaw, thumb, thigh, thought, three, throne.

Sounded as *dhr* in They, thee, than, then, this, though, thus, thy, thine, thou.

" " *s* " Say, see, sad, soon, set, saw, sigh, soil, sue, so.

" " *z* " Zero, zest, zone, zebra, zeal, zigzag, zealot, zenith, zephyr, zany.

" " *sh* " Shark, shape, sheep, shall, show, shell, ship, shoe, shoot, shawl.

" " *zh* " Azure, vision, collision, leisure, measure, collusion, seizure, pleasure.

" " *m* " Ma, may, meek, map, met, mud, Maud, mope, moon, mind.

" " *n* " Nay, neat, nap, net, no, noon, nod, nook, nor, nudge.

" " *ing* " Ring, bring, sing, fling, rang, bang, sung, wing, lung, young.

" " *l* " Lay, lard, leap, lap, lid, law, live, low, (Struck up) loop, lug.

" " *r* " Bar, tear, fair, her, jar, or, oar, fur, pure, near.

" " *r* " Rake, read, rack, red, rig, raw, rule, rod, (Struck up) rub, roll.

" " *w* " Wad, wake, week, wag, wit, wedge, wall, wove, wool, wide.

" " *y* " Yarn, yea, year, yet, yes, yeast, you, yoke, yield, yore.

" " *h* " Hay, heap, hat, ham, hot, hoe, hall, hood, hut, hill.

All consonant stems, except Ree, are derived from the following circles:

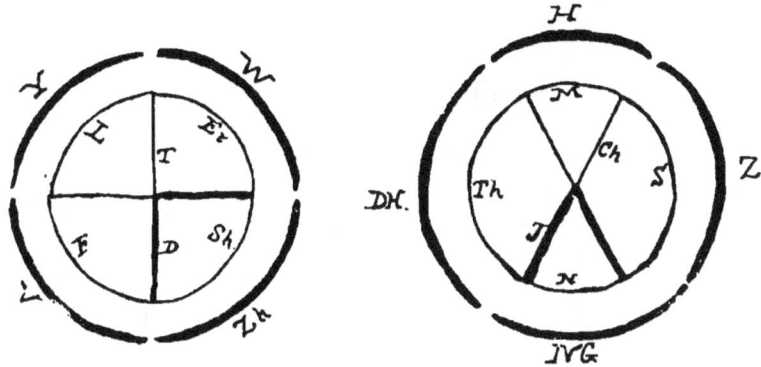

All perpendicular or inclined stems are written downward, except L and Ree.

Horizontal stems are written from left to right.

R, when preceded by a vowel, has the sound of Er—as, *oar* and *or;* but when used at the beginning of a word, it has the sound of Ree—as, *rod* and *ray.*

Ree is always written upward, and stands at an angle midway between CH and K: thus:

VOWELS.

Vowels are indicated by three each light and heavy dots, and light and heavy dashes. These are distinguished by being placed at the *beginning, middle,* and *end* of stem for *first, second,* and *third place* vowels.

SIMPLE VOWELS.

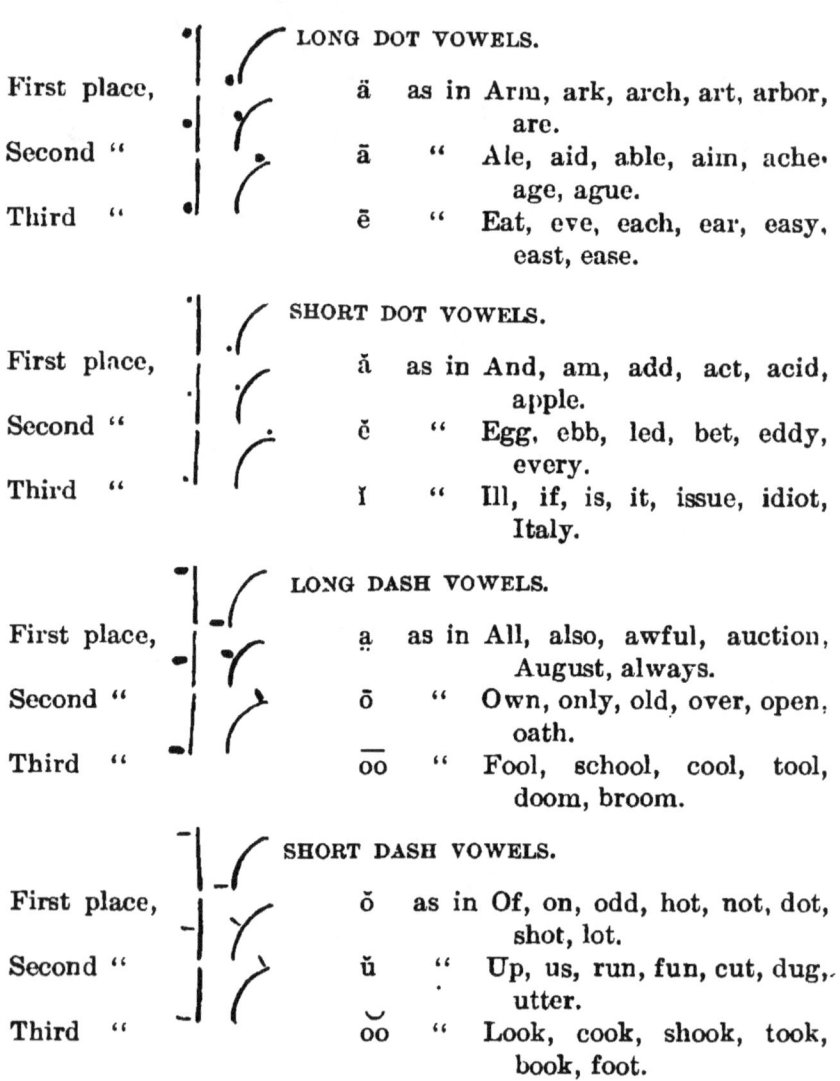

LONG DOT VOWELS.

First place,   ä   as in Arm, ark, arch, art, arbor, are.
Second "   ā   "   Ale, aid, able, aim, ache, age, ague.
Third "   ē   "   Eat, eve, each, ear, easy, east, ease.

SHORT DOT VOWELS.

First place,   ă   as in And, am, add, act, acid, apple.
Second "   ĕ   "   Egg, ebb, led, bet, eddy, every.
Third "   ĭ   "   Ill, if, is, it, issue, idiot, Italy.

LONG DASH VOWELS.

First place,   a̤   as in All, also, awful, auction, August, always.
Second "   ō   "   Own, only, old, over, open, oath.
Third "   ōō   "   Fool, school, cool, tool, doom, broom.

SHORT DASH VOWELS.

First place,   ŏ   as in Of, on, odd, hot, not, dot, shot, lot.
Second "   ŭ   "   Up, us, run, fun, cut, dug, utter.
Third "   ŏŏ   "   Look, cook, shook, took, book, foot.

SUPPLEMENTARY LESSONS.

DIPHTHONGS OR DOUBLE VOWELS.

First place, ⎯ ᵛ| ᵥ⌒ ī as in Ice, ire, item, ivy, iron, idle.
"   "   ⎯ ᑉ| ᑉ⌒ oi "   Toy, boil, coin, foil, oily, oyster.
"   "   ⎯ ᒪ| ᒪ⌒ ow "   Cow, how, now, out, hour, sour.
Third "   ⎯ ᶻ| ᶻ⌒ ū "   Few, sue, knew, cube, pure, fuel.

Diphthongs should always point in the proper direction, regardless of the form of the stem.

In writing a word, the consonant stem is always written first.

Order of reading: Vowels placed to perpendicular or inclined stems are read from left to right, as in longhand; when placed to horizontals, they are read from top to bottom.

CAUTION.—The *point of beginning* of any *stem* is always *first* vowel place; the middle, second place; and the end, third place.

When two vowels occur together, either before or after a consonant stem, the vowel which is *read* next to the stem is placed *nearest* it.

CONSONANT POSITIONS.

The consonant stem has three positions with respect to line of writing.

The position of consonant stem is governed by the *place* of vowel.

If there is more than one vowel, the consonant must agree with the *accented* vowel.

FIRST position of *all* stems is above the line.

SECOND position of *all* stems, on the line.

THIRD position of *perpendicular* or *inclined* stems, halfway through the line.

THIRD position of *horizontal* stems, entirely below the line.

Therefore, in writing a word, we have to consider:
1st. The vowel and its place.
2d. Write the stem in its proper position to agree with the vowel, or with the *accented* vowel if there be more than one.
3d. Place the vowel to the stem.

A dash vowel should be written at a right angle with that part of stem at which it is written.

ONE CONSONANT WORDS.

aid	Poe	egg	die	shy	out
gnaw	eke	it	chew	my	Ike
yea	sea	on	joy	mow	easy
woo	paw	us	Jew	nigh	airy
ray	each	of	cow	now	any
or	do	up	cue	mew	alloy
ye	lea	ash	fie	new	issue
ease	eel	ebb	few	lie	Amy
thee	go	if	vie	ire	alley
she	two	air	vow	our	era
ooze	ear	edge	view	wry	essay
knee	tea	Ann	thy	row	allow
ought	know	ell	sigh	how	echo
fee	am	pie	sue	high	Eva

SUPPLEMENTARY LESSONS.

CONTRACTIONS.

An or and.............A.................the.................

I or of.................awe................Oh or owe..............

as or has.............is or his..............self.................

to or too.............who, whom................................

SENTENCES.

It is day now, and you may row on the bay.
The ice may thaw if we go on it.
She may be away, or she may be ill.
I may pay all I owe in a day or so.
On any day you may see us in the alley.
Is Eddie in Ohio now or in Iowa?
The hour is up and you may go away.
Ella and Addie may go out to tea if we do.
If I am away on the sea, you may be too.
I am to pay you if you aid me in any way.
You may die if you eat pie, though you may eat an egg.
The oak and ash are up high in the air.
Though we are so easy, we may sue you ere you go away, and you pay the fee.
Now the cow is at the hay mow. Is it my cow? You ought to know, as you saw it.
May thy way be all joy.

LESSON IV.

Two or more consonant stems may be joined (without removing the pencil), writing the stems in the same direction as when alone, and placing the vowels to the consonants.

When two curved stems, derived from the *same* circle, naturally forming a semicircle, are joined, there should be *no* angle between them; except H and S. These require a slight angle in order to make the latter stem sufficiently light.

When two curves derived from *different* circles are joined, there *should be* an angle between them. (See page 5.)

The position of the *first* perpendicular or inclined stem in a word must agree with the *accented* vowel.

Vowels occurring between two stems are placed as follows:

All *first* place and *long* second place are written to the stem which precedes the vowel.

All *third* place and *short* second place are written to the stem which *follows* the vowel.

ORDER OF WRITING.

1st. Determine the *accented* vowel.
2d. Write outline so that the position of the *first* perpendicular or inclined stem shall agree with the accented vowel.
3d. Place the vowels to the stems according to above rules.

ORDER OF READING.

The same as when only one stem is used—perpendicular or inclined stems from left to right, and horizontals from top to bottom.

take	package	following
like	period	managing
enjoy	readily	apology
vouch	touching	making
deny	deeming	keeping
both	joking	catching
cash	month	topic
laying	unfair	to-morrow
although	pushing	attaching
shape	voyaging	deputy
big	foaming	ingenuity
delay	matching	alleging

SENTENCES.

Do you enjoy life, or are you in a hurry to be rich?
The book is read by old and young.
We rode an hour in the park, and saw many we knew.
Do you know how deep the lake is, and how long?
Being weary, I lay in the hammock all day, and read the book you liked so much.
Take a walk on the beach and out on the pier, and look at the sea.
You ought to be laying up money for a rainy day.
It is unfair to ask me to pay you the cash to-morrow, although I may do so.
Do you enjoy fishing as much as you like fish? I do if I am catching any.

LESSON V.

With a few exceptions a small circle may be substituted for the stem signs S and Z.

The circle should be written on the *right* side of *straight* perpendicular or inclined stems, on the upper side of *straight* horizontals, and *inside* of curved stems.

The circle should be written to Ree the same as K and G.

No vowel can precede an initial circle, nor follow a final one.

INITIAL CIRCLE.

soon	specie	speedy
sick	swim	suiting
sail	sneak	scheme
some	sealing	Senate
slowly	solid	signing
sweep	Sunday	ceremony
saving	safety	summary

FINAL CIRCLE.

miss	items	rejoice
knows	always	appears
nice	theories	anxious
does	repose	advice
peace	invoice	cautious
gaze	notice	cheapness
loose	famous	thickness
this	device	announce
guess	makes	minus
mix	knocks	annex
tax	refuse	follows
hums	copies	induce

SUPPLEMENTARY LESSONS.

INITIAL AND FINAL CIRCLES.

signs	sleeps	surveys
sales	speeches	slowness
seeds	sketches	smokes
suppose	sadness	sickness
six	swings	spheres
sums	snaps	sweeps

S CIRCLE BETWEEN STEMS.

When two straight stems are struck in the same direction, the circle should be written as to one stem.

| tacit | tasty | Tuesday |
| resource | deceit | outside |

The circle should be written *outside* the *angle* between two straight stems, forming an angle at their junction.

besides	despise	expose	exceeding
upset	receipt	discuss	dispatch
beseech	disobey	opposite	laxity
succeed	sixty	dispose	disappear
episode	disguise	bestow	custody
deposit	reside	sagacity	injustice

If one or both are curved stems, the circle should be written *inside* the curve.

chosen	business	facing
desire	receives	losing
dozen	passing	facile
honesty	pacify	vessel
specifies	sincere	fasten
answers	insight	using
absence	hasty	refusing
ensued	opposing	salesman
reason	associate	vicinity
dismiss	raising	enthusiasm
disease	music	dishonesty
causing	soliciting	Messrs.

Between two curved stems struck in *opposite* directions, the circle should be written inside the *first* curve.

lesson	amazing	hasten
moisten	losing	amusing
license	amassing	masonic

Between two curves struck in opposite directions, and forming an acute angle, the circle should be turned *outside* the angle.

| nicely | facility |
| vacillate | unsullied |

LESSON VI.

EXCEPTIONS TO THE USE OF *S* CIRCLE.

Always use the S or Z stem when it is preceded or followed by *two concurrent* vowels.

saying	joyous	curious
seeing	sewer	spurious
sighing	essaying	ingenuous
miasma	fatuous	museum

Use the S or Z stem when it is the *first* consonant *preceded* by a vowel; or, the *last* consonant *followed* by a vowel.

assets	also	uneasy
asking	racy	Lucy
acid	dizzy	tipsy
asleep	fussy	ecstasy
aspire	spicy	efficacy
eyesight	cozy	policy
assignee	busy	pursue
essence	noisy	accuracy
usurp	rosy	solvency

Always use Z stem when it is the *first* consonant in a word.

zone	zealot	Ezra
easiness	zoology	zealous

LARGE CIRCLE.

When two *s* or *z* sounds occur together, with only a vowel between them, a large circle may be used in same manner as small one; and, if the vowel is *accented*, it may be written inside the circle.

season	cases	voices
sausage	supposes	induces
success	races	taxes

boxes	forces	desist
rises	exposes	necessary
faces	devices	excessive
masses	resources	insist
analysis	exercise	successors
notices	emphasis	precisely

SMALL LOOP.

The sound of *st* or *zd* may be represented by a small loop, written on the circle side, and extending one-third the length of the stem. This loop may be used initially, finally or in the middle of words.

In the *middle* of words, the stem should be crossed in writing a circle, but *not* in writing a loop.

stops	zest	disposed	honestly
sticks	west	copyist	jesting
steer	forced	advised	testing
states	taxed	fixed	vastly
stoves	utmost	noticed	destiny
stale	reposed	mixed	tasting
statue	oldest	annexed	costly
steaming	refused	incased	justness
stealing	earliest	induced	earnestly
studying	mixed	unjust	adjusting

LARGE LOOP.

The *ster* sound is represented by a large loop extending two-thirds the length of the stem. This is never used at the beginning of words.

foster	monster	songster
lustre	register	mastering
coaster	teamster	lobster
vaster	sinister	disturb

A small *s* or *z* circle may be added to the large circle, or either of the loops, by crossing the stem and placing the circle on the opposite side.

excesses	costs	posters
recesses	wastes	fosters
exercises	hosts	masters

LESSON VII.

L or R (Ree) stem is struck *upward* when it is the *first* sound in the word; and *downward* (Er) when it is the *last* sound in the word.

up	L	down	up	R	down
like		foul	rush		chair
lack		guile	rob		tire
lake		toll	renew		fair
lime		fail	wreck		poor
leak		pole	retail		bore
loom		tale	ruinous		adore
log		foil	receive		fire
lame		peal	rainy		tower
lucky		vile	refuse		pour
lamb		appall	reposed		fear
league		disposal	renewal		lower

L or R (Ree) is struck *upward* when it is the *last* consonant in a word *followed* by a *vowel*.

L		R	
mellow	rally	borrow	thorough
follow	lowly	worry	hurry
lily	relay	merry	jury
billow	below	bowery	vary
July	shyly	marry	ferry
daily	duly	dowry	ivory
rely	highly	morrow	tarry
chilly	outlay	fairy	dairy

L is struck *upward* when it is the *only* stem in a word.

ill	allay	oil	Ella
eel	lieu	low	isle
seal	slow	silly	alley
lease	loss	laws	last
loose	lies	least	allays

L is struck *upward* when followed by a *down* stroke (*e. g.*, throwing a ball in the air; it must be thrown up in order to come down).

life	leave	lobby	levy
aloof	always	latch	lodge
elope	leap	loath	loaf
elegy	live	ledge	allowed

R (Er) is always struck downward when it is the first or only consonant *preceded* by a *vowel*.

array	argue	earnestly
sir	early	earlier
arouse	airily	seriously

Downstroke L when preceded by a vowel *and* followed by a horizontal stem.

| ailing | Elmira | allegory |
| elect | allowance | alumni |

Downstroke L when followed by MP or MB.

| lamp | limp | lumpy | limbo | lymph |

Downstroke R (Er) when followed by M or H.

| rim | aroma | room | rummage |
| arming | ceremony | remedy | remove |

Upstroke R (Ree) when followed by TH, DH, CH, J.

wreathe	ridge	righteous
richly	rejoiced	register
arching	raging	archly
rhythm	regimen	Ruth

In the middle of words, upstroke R and L are preferred.

carrying	worrying	dilemma	following
horrify	verify	delaying	relying
March	outrage	mollify	mileage
territory	borrowing	Italic	unload

LESSON VIII.

The *l* or *r* sound, when immediately following another consonant, is indicated by a hook written at the beginning of the stem it follows.

On *straight* stems, a small hook for *l* is placed on the right or circle side of the stem; the *r* hook, on the opposite side.

On *curved* stems, a *large* hook at the beginning, and turned inside the stem, is used for *l*, and a *small* hook for *r*.

The hook is always written first, but it is read *after* the stem.

STRAIGHT STEMS WITH *L* AND *R* HOOKS.

L		R	
closed	black	address	prejudice
glee.	click	praise	precisely
place	pluck	drop	promise
classes	gleam	prices	protest
oral	oblige	trusting	pressing
blaze	claims	tracer	groceries
please	pledge	produce	presume
glazed	cloth	previous	premium
agile	clear	proposes	price-list
glass	placing	proceeds	criticism
plaster	dealer	breath	precious
bluster	climax	trunk	previously
globe	blame	trial	predecessor

CURVED STEMS WITH *L* AND *R* HOOKS.

L		R	
easily	unless	affray	energy
oval	floor	inner	freely
evil	only	every	France
easel	flowers	over	Friday
flies		others	

L AND *R* HOOKS IN THE MIDDLE OF WORDS.

L		R	
deeply	legible	powder	sundries
suitable	pitiful	liberal	voucher
original	desirable	neighbor	intrust
chiefly	negotiable	betray	increasing

SUPPLEMENTARY LESSONS.

L		R	
double	bushel	dinner	richer
pickle	channel	defray	repress
joyful	shovel	keeper	generosity
final	weekly	ledger	loafer
staple	local	maker	depressed
implies	employers	favor	figure
enables	likely	colors	vigorous
simply	implicit	astray	archery
ample	reasonable	erasure	wager
noble	libel	impressing	embraced
legal	samples	inferior	defer
assembly	lawful	measure	pleasure
level	arrival	impoverish	censure
inclosed	payable	newspaper	minor
unjustifiable	vocal	slumbers	banner
enviable	muzzle	winner	deference
removal	feeble	robbery	numerous
audibly	capable	liberty	thinner
ridicule	obstacle	lunar	embroidery

MEDIAL HOOK FORMED BY RETRACING PRECEDING STEM.

L		R	
replace	reply	joker	digger
circles	cable	ticker	poodle
couple	reclaims	packer	depressed
rebel	gable	progress	weaker

L AND R HOOKS ON BOTH STEMS.

playful	honorable	marvel
plainly	troubles	privileges
glazier	treasure	criminal
glimmer	pressure	traveling
flicker	preference	fresher
plainer	trifle	braver
fulfilling	driver	preacher
pleasure	agreeable	brokerage

WORDS IN WHICH THE REL IS USED.

girl	narrowly	necessarily
hurl	nearly	sincerely
merely	clearly	demoralized
plural	wearily	thoroughly

LESSON IX.

SPECIAL VOCALIZATION.

The *r* or *l* hook may sometimes be used when there is a distinct vowel intervening, and the vowel written as follows:

The *heavy* dot vowel, by a small circle placed *before* the stem in its proper place.

The *light* dot vowel, by a small circle placed *after* the stem.

The *stronger*, or heavy dot, naturally preceding the stem, and the *weaker*, or light dot, following.

The dash vowels and diphthongs are struck across the stems, or at the end if they interfere with a hook.

DOT VOWELS, SPECIAL VOCALIZATION.

rail	bearers	perceive	impoverish
hill	failure	defer	engineers
cheer	partial	average	adversity
deal	daring	ability	terminal
aware	charity	mailing	telegrams
feel	nervous	pioneer	proposal
nearest	cheerful	anarchy	mercury
jar	harbor	penalty	calumny
wail	valuable	eternal	preferring
averse	earner	prefer	liberal
nail	philosophy	careful	telescope
dark	relate	embarrassed	parlor
verge	reliable	energy	harmony
terms	parties	rarely	parsimony
harm	person	releasing	charming
germ	wearing	welfare	preparing
harsh	careless	generous	farming
jerk	parcel	marvel	overwhelm

DASH VOWELS AND DIPHTHONGS, SPECIAL VOCALIZATION.

wool	murmur	nullify	falseness
core	nourish	enormous	figure
mire	colonize	purchase	retire
hole	incur	assurance	befallen
burst	wholesale	apologize	indorsed
yore	ignore	procure	encouraging
cool	empire	occurrences	censure
dull	warm	former	reimburse
curse	recur	authority	courtesy
worse	journal	falling	cordially
coal	vulgar	rulable	collateral
horse	normal	surety	journeying
nurse	fulfill	foreign	purchaser
north	ridicule	recourse	temporarily

A small circle may be placed on any hook, and is always read first.

suffer	cycle	school
small	sooner	civilized
cipher	sickly	severity
subtle	sever	suffrage

S CIRCLE AND HOOKS IN THE MIDDLE OF WORDS.

peacefully	possible	personal
plausible	dishonorable	physical
prisoner	displeasing	adducible
deceiver	fusible	noticeable

Instead of writing the *s* circle *on* the *r* hook, the hook may be shown by writing the *s* circle on the *r* side of STRAIGHT stems. The large circle and *st* loop may also be written in the same way. This class of words is called the *sper* series.

sadder	cedar	strides
sicker	scoring	stream
solder	scourge	strong

struck	string	strenuous
strike	scarcity	scrupulous
stroke	security	sacrifice
striker	spread	struggling
struggle	scarcely	superior
storms	spring	supreme

S CIRCLE ON R HOOK SIDE OF STEMS IN THE MIDDLE OF WORDS.

destroying	disgracing	descry
disasterous	prosperity	etcetera
discouraging	prosperous	discourse
obscurely	disagreeably	distressing

WORDS IN WHICH BOTH R HOOK AND S CIRCLE MUST APPEAR.

mystery	restore	solicitor
extremely	expressed	mastery
external	expiring	inextricably
registry	expressage	ministry
hysterical	massacre	posterity
restrict	vesper	masker

An initial *large* hook on the circle or *l* hook side of *straight* stems, may be used for the consonant W.

quick	quiver	bequeath
quiz	quickly	twinkle
quoth	quicker	quench
quite	quietness	acquiesce
queer	twirl	squalor
queerly	inquiry	requisite
query	sanguinary	inadequacy

In, en, un, may be prefixed to stems with an initial circle by crossing the stem with a little curl.

unseemly	unsafe	unsullied
enslaves	inspirable	insatiable
insular	insoluble	unceremonious
enseal	unsalable	unscrupulous

The *y* hook, a large hook on *r* side of straight stems, is only used in phrasing.

LESSON X.

F AND V HOOKS.

Consonants *f* or *v* may be added to any *straight* stem by a small *final* hook on the right or circle side, the hook being read after the stem and its vowels. This hook may also be used in the middle of words.

curve	paving	river	graphic
brief	cover	divine	reverses
cliff	defense	puffing	discover
groove	devoid	toughen	devote
engrave	proving	chafing	refreshing
deprive	driving	traffic	improving
deserve	braving	provoke	depraving
positive	diving	driven	stenographic
tariff	telephone	advanced	undeviating

A long *narrow* final hook may be used for *f* or *v* on *curved* stems, but, like the *y* hook, it is only used in phrasing.

N HOOK.

Consonant *n* is indicated by a *small* final hook on the left or *r* hook side of *straight* stems, and by a *small* final hook inside *curved* stems. Also used in the middle of words.

grain	one	obtain	bargain
drawn	deepen	pardon	sermon
down	detain	beaten	specimen
clean	refine	tighten	examine
keen	broken	uneven	retain
join	incline	regain	engine
upon	remain	origin	outdone
session	taken	weaken	turn

SUPPLEMENTARY LESSONS.   25

enjoin	slacken	unknown	cotton
reckon	discern	imagine	recline
routine	enshrine	machine	quicken
rejoin	marine	pertain	margin
women	discipline	brighten	unshaken

THE N HOOK IN THE MIDDLE OF WORDS.

strange	training	opening	vacancy
plunge	planning	beneath	emergency
earning	plenty	shining	tremendous
gainsay	assigning	vanish	unanimity
evening	dawning	turning	remaining
punish	banish	frowning	genuineness
manifest	branches	furnish	declining
learning	abandon	morning	merchandise
warning	finances	canvassed	mechanics
union	unite	gaining	impertinence
fancy	arrange	urgency	examining
drainage	guarantee	monopoly	retrench
reckoning	obtaining	occupancy	strenuous
gleaning	penman	discrepancy	detaining
brandy	oranges	economical	ascertaining
greenings	Monday	universal	obstinately
running	evening	patronage	leniency

Words which should be written with the F, V, or N stem, because it is followed by a vowel:

defy	avenue	bony	irony
puffy	coney	honey	rainy
bevy	tiny	stony	mutiny
typify	pony	deny	alimony
terrify	ebony	renew	assignee
purify	canoe	felony	venue
deify	brawny	crony	arena
exemplify	revenue	Tammany	villainy

SUPPLEMENTARY LESSONS.

Syllables *shun* or *zhun* may be added by a *large final* hook on the circle or *f* hook side of *straight* stems, and a large final hook on *curved* stems.

portion	violation	erection
suspicion	supervision	precaution
aversion	reaction	stagnation
solution	elevation	provision
seclusion	election	allegation
sanction	petition	variation
situation	adoption	devotion
duration	occupation	ambition
oppression	instruction	exertion
section	definition	supplication
nation	appreciation	calculations
omission	solicitation	restriction
attention	destination	circulation
suspension	perfection	prosecution
foundation	prostration	discretion
deliberation	desperation	incorporation
mention	remission	distribution
expression	quotation	declaration
opperation	speculation	litigation
dissolution	impression	elimination
exertion	reduction	classification
execution	proportion	negotiation
selection	humiliation	liquidation
restoration	repetition	reflection
assertion	destruction	extrication
regulation	observation	specification
desertion	institution	fluctuation
destination	importation	discrimination
corporation	expiration	injunction
location	presentation	reputation
attraction	examination	accumulation
rejection	inclination	nomination
obligation	determination	imagination

Shun Curl.—To a word having a final *circle*, the *shun* or *zhun* may be added by crossing the stem with a little curl.

causation	proposition
opposition	imposition
acquisition	indecision
succession	exposition
disposition	incision
procession	taxation
association	vexation
realization	deposition
accusation	transposition
pulsation	indisposition

Syllables *ter, ther, dhr,* may be added to any *straight* stem by a *large* final hook on the left or *n* hook side.

Caution.—This hook is never used for *der* on *straight* stems.

better	creator	charter
actor	clatter	creditor
pewter	starter	executor
tutor	spatter	corporator
gutter	greater	speculator
brighter	brother	typewriter
rather	traitor	proprietor

This hook may be used for *ture,* and the diphthong placed inside the hook.

picture	creature	departure
culture	rupture	fracture

A small circle may be added to any final hook or *shun* curl.

cuffs	roofs	dives	thence
gloves	coves	grieves	assigns
roves	chafes	hence	lines

earns	omissions	petitions	gathers
yawns	portions	positions	daughters
once	editions	chatters	tatters
arraigns	patience	creatures	barters
orations	occupations	caters	charters

When *s* follows *n* hook, the circle may be turned on *n* hook side of the stem, as in the *sper* series. The large circle and loops may also be used in this manner.

rains	chains	balance	guidance
beans	tunes	obtains	dispense
opens	joins	expense	assistance
pains	towns	response	expenses
duns	gains	residence	acceptance
tons	canister	pertains	negligence
scorns	banister	elegance	existence

S ON *N* SIDE IN MIDDLE OF WORDS.

dancing	prancing	expensive
balancing	transfuse	transfix

LARGE FINAL HOOKS IN THE MIDDLE OF WORDS.

stationary	gathering
exceptional	capturing
motioning	bothering
traditional	bitterness
missionary	scattering
auctioneer	caterer
cautionary	battering
fractional	sputterer
deficiency	rhetoric

LESSON XI.

Ter, der, thr, dhr, is added to a *curved* stem by doubling its length.

Positions for *downward* double-length stems:

1st. On the line.

2d. Halfway through the line.

3d. Two-thirds below the line.

A straight stem may be lengthened to add above sounds, *if it has a final hook.*

The *ter, der, thr, dhr*, is the last sound to be read, unless there be a final circle.

enter	interview	materially
shudder	fatherly	elevators
wider	altering	intercourse
future	interfere	astronomy
lighter	laughter	furtherance
ardor	interval	signature
sounder	underlay	janitor
holders	undergo	interruption
lenders	maturity	underselling
falter	intersection	defaulter
interests	literally	prematurely
underpay	austerity	international

STRAIGHT STEMS WITH FINAL HOOKS LENGTHENED.

splinters	plundering	rendering
pondering	counteraction	blunderer
pointers	counterpane	tenderness

LESSONS XII. AND XIII.

Writing any consonant half-length adds *t* or *d*.

The *third* position of a half-length *perpendicular* or inclined stem is *entirely* below the line. The other positions are unchanged.

The *t* or *d* is the last sound to be read, unless there be a final circle.

ONE STEM HALF-LENGTH.

get	tried	brand
taught	hand	draft
bought	find	amount
cheat	fault	seconds
goods	bounds	secured

LAST STEM HALF-LENGTH.

prompt	apparent	measured	repaired
strict	upwards	per cent	temperate
enabled	resort	excellent	repugnant
market	merchants	perfect	duplicate
absent	incurred	disappoint	product
agent	refund	president	discounts
instant	hesitate	remind	shipments
delight	appreciate	accident	assistant
result	retained	settlements	documents
except	deferred	desperate	henceforward
present	tenant	judgment	extricate
imports	deprived	illustrate	equivalent
demands	expend	bereavement	improvement
thousand	recent	afterward	disinclined
remind	warrant	stipulate	environment
exclude	payments	deponent	remunerate
extend	statements	recuperate	assessments
expect	current	engaged	reimbursement
retired	remit	district	indorsement

SUPPLEMENTARY LESSONS.

FIRST STEM HALF-LENGTH.

getting	October	estimation	anticipation
little	greatly	naturally	intentional
lately	gradually	articles	tendency
letting	relative	country	metropolis
actually	ordinary	kindly	indulgence
mutually	pointing	modern	maintaining
modify	central	printing	countenance
witness	counting	intentions	threatening
actively	pending	maintain	accordance
evidence	handle	friendly	quantity
catalogue	gratifies	suspending	spiritual
grandly	standing	lunatic	assorting

BOTH STEMS HALF-LENGTH.

notified	lightened	indebted
meditate	modified	participate
moderate	estimates	anticipate
intimate	treatment	protested
esteemed	credited	assortment
astound	threatened	multiplied
ratified	candidate	intestate
eradicate	intend	standard

MIDDLE STEM HALF-LENGTH.

entitle	capital	defective
pocketing	obliterate	accumulating
remodeling	delighting	obviating
coveting	legitimate	piloting
vividly	evidently	alternative
enacting	responding	uncertain
rapidly	politely	indebtedness
promptly	regarding	individual
inviting	acceptable	instantaneous
resorting	apparently	indefinitely
rectify	dependence	correspondence
erecting	defending	speculative
rejecting	negotiating	inventory

misfortunes	lucrative	agricultural
mercantile	Atlantic	agriculturist
remittances	political	disappointment
remunerative	profoundly	fraudulently
perfectly	inevitable	misunderstanding

Caution.—When full and half length stems do not form an angle at their junction, both stems must be written in full.

liked	locked	barbed
cooked	kicked	category
clicked	forked	catechise
corked	victim	victory
looked	octagon	inculcate

All words ending in *ted* or *ded must* be written with the half-length T or D.

acted	handed	pointed
cheated	attended	assorted
guided	elected	terminated
fitted	branded	depreciated
voted	merited	expended
noted	deluded	reported
lighted	delighted	departed
rated	intended	intrusted
pleaded	indicated	assaulted
lifted	moderated	asserted
located	detected	separated
rented	estimated	ungranted
repeated	corrected	prevented
adapted	printed	superseded
defrauded	emitted	succeeded

Half-length T or D may be detached and written near the preceding stem, if, when joined, it does not form an angle.

dotted	awarded	worded
dreaded	entreated	persuaded
undoubted	destitute	retreated
institute	necessitated	liquidated
doted	substituted	hesitated

SUPPLEMENTARY LESSONS.

Final T and D, like the S stem, must be written in full when followed by a vowel.

duty	shadow	ready
pity	meadow	outdo
beauty	shoddy	lady
needy	haughty	deduce
oddity	tidy	entice
naughty	muddy	flighty
empty	reduce	hardy
veto	moody	verity
mighty	ditto	penalty
data	body	giddy

L or Ree, when *only* stem in the word, is made half-length to add *t*, and full length with the D stem to add *d*.

light—lied	late—laid
rot—rod	let—load
writ—read	lout—loud
lot—lad	lute—lid
rate—raid	wrote—rowed
rut—red	lit—allude
lute—lead	slight—slide
root—rude	slate—sled
route—rid	slit—sealed

When T or D is preceded by *two* vowels, the full stem must be used.

poet	diet	quiet
riot	laity	fiat
	reiterate	

When the present tense of a verb is written with a *double* length stem, it is sometimes better to form the past tense by adding a T or D stem than to make both stems half-length. The original outline of the word should always be preserved as nearly as possible.

squander-ed	hinder-ed
render-ed	surrender-ed
wonder-ed	plunder-ed
blunder-ed	slander-ed
flounder-ed	shelter-ed

LESSON XIV.

The consonant *h* may sometimes be omitted, and indicated by a small dot placed before the vowel.

hoop	heavy	unhitch
hopes	hoof	unhinge
hopeless	happen	hopped
heave	behoof	having
hip	heaped	handkerchief
hobby	hived	habituate
unhappy	help	happens

H sounded before consonant *w* may be indicated by prefixing an upright tick to the W stem.

whist	whipped	whaler
whisk	whine	whittle
while	whitecap	whitewash

W AND Y BRIEF SIGNS.

W brief is a small semicircle opening to the right or left; and *Y* brief, opening upward or downward.

wipe	wives	watchman	euphony
wood	without	wishing	Europe
weighty	waving	yoke	eulogy
weave	winked	yelp	utensil

Final syllables *ly* and *ry* may be written with the *l* and *r* hooks when there is no distinct vowel between the stem and hook.

LY

nominally	thickly	clearly
finally	exceedingly	necessarily
mainly	annoyingly	radically
legally	certainly	melancholy
firmly	officially	sincerely
rashly	cheerfully	overwhelmingly
initially	partially	positively
busily	playfully	charmingly
calmly	cozily	grudgingly
lively	wrongly	faithfully
deeply	suddenly	personally
cheaply	likely	thoroughly
namely	squarely	unusually

RY

robbery	mockery	slippery
crockery	bakery	seminary
treasury	bribery	surgery

Sometimes the last stem in a word may be made half-length to add *ty*.

integrity	inability	credibility
majority	possibility	liability
legality	quality	acceptability
suitability	respectability	mutability

LESSON XV.

SENTENCES WITH WORD SIGNS.

"All would live long, but none would be old."—*B. Franklin.*

"All men have their price."—*Walpole.*

"He was not for an age, but for all time."—*B. Jonson, of Shakespeare.*

"There never was a night that had no morn."—*D. M. Mulock.*

"I have sent for you, that you may see how a Christian can die."—*Addison.*

"I have begun several times many things, and have often succeeded at last. I will sit down now, but the time will come when you will hear me."—*Disraeli.*

"They have been at a great feast of languages, and stolen the scraps."—*Love's Labor Lost.*

"Never spend your money before you have it. Never buy what you do not want because it is cheap. When angry, count ten before you speak; if very angry, count a hundred."—*Jefferson's Ten Rules.*

"These are the times that try men's souls."—*T. Paine.*

"We have met the enemy, and they are ours."—*Com. Perry.*

"I know not what course others may take; but as for me, give me liberty, or give me death."—*Patrick Henry.*

"What would you do if you were in our place?"—*Gen. Lee.*

"Desire not to live long, but to live well:
How long we live, not years, but actions tell."
—*Shakespeare.*

"Every age, race, and condition has been marked by the hope of an existence reaching beyond this life into another and better one."

"The Egyptians practiced embalming because of their belief that the body would be resurrected entire, as at death."

"There are nearly three thousand languages in the world, but many of them so similar that they may be considered as dialects of the same language."

" The friends who in our sunshine live,
  When winter comes are flown ;
  And he who has but tears to give
  Must weep those tears alone."
                        —*Thomas Moore.*

" No man e'er felt the halter draw, with good opinion of the law."—*John Trumbull.*

" An honest man's the noblest work of God."—*Pope.*

" There are many people who think that Sunday is a sponge to wipe out all the sins of the week."—*H. W. Beecher.*

" The Almighty Dollar, that great object of universal devotion."—*W. Irving.*

" The half was not told me." " As far as the east is from the west." " Let another man praise thee, and not thine own mouth." " Answer not a fool according to his folly." " There is no new thing under the sun."—*Bible.*

" First in war, first in peace, first in the hearts of his fellow-citizens."—*Gen. Lee, of Washington.*

" Distinct as the billows, yet one as the ocean."—*Daniel Webster.*

" There is no why without a *because*." " The world exists for the education of each man. There is no age or state of society, or mode of action in history, to which there is not somewhat corresponding in his life."—*Emerson.*

" To be pleasant, one must please. What pleases you in others, will in general please them in you." " Every man seeks for the truth : God only knows who has found it."—*Lord Chesterfield.*

" Come wealth or want, come good or ill,
  Let young and old accept their part,
  And bow before the awful will,
  And bear it with an honest heart.
  Who misses, or who wins the prize,—
    Go, lose or conquer as you can ;
  But if you fail, or if you rise,
    Be each, pray God, a gentleman."
                        —*Thackeray.*

LESSON XVI.

CONTRACTIONS.

Prefixes are indicated as follows:
Com, con, cum, cog, may be omitted, and shown by placing the remainder of the word in *proximity* to the preceding word or syllable.

If impossible to denote by proximity, a dot may be written before and at the end of the following stem in place of either of these syllables.

COM.

complain	commission	compilation
commonest	community	commercial
composing	compromise	communicating
completion	compete	compliance
commend	completed	recommit
competency	compatible	incompetent
comparatively	comprise	unaccompanied
competent	complimentary	uncompromising
complicate	comprehend	discommode
combination	commencement	incomplete
compose	compensation	accommodations
compare	compression	recompense
commences	commendable	incomprehensible
compliment	complexion	accomplish
complying	complaint	accommodate
compels	complete	recommends
commander	communication	incomprehensive
commence	competitors	discomposure

CON.

consent	conversation	confirm
confer	contrives	confining
connection	concur	confronted
contain	contents	conclusively
concession	consideration	conference
consist	conducted	contribute
contends	control	confidently
conclusions	contrary	concurrence

SUPPLEMENTARY LESSONS.

continue	consignees	unreconciled
commodity	continuing	disconnect
construction	consequently	unconfined
consciousness	constituents	unconscious
consignment	concentrated	inconstant
congratulation	unconcern	inconsistent
concerning	incongruity	reconcile
convenience	reconsider	discontinue
conscientious	uncontroverted	discontent
considerable	unconditional	disconcert
contingency	inconsiderate	inconvenience
confidential	reconstruct	inconsolable
consistency	uncontrolled	inconsequent

CUM

cumbrous	cumbrance	recumbent
cumbrously	circumspect	circumspection
comfort	discomfort	discomfiture
compass	encompassed	company

PROXIMITY PHRASES.

under control	no comparison
you consider	excellent composition
very comfortable	perfect control
liberal contribution	nearly completed
well connected	always contending
we concede	naturally contain
great conflict	recent conference
large congregation	people congregate
they console	simple construction
in consequence	deliberate consideration
authors contribute	personally conducted
their confidence	earliest convenience
now complaining	direct communication
your consent	beautiful combination
in connection	close confinement
our company	full confession
must contrive	please consult
please consult	these complicated conditions
in compliance	they command complete
will confer	confidence

Common sense is called common by common consent, but it is the scarcest commodity in the market.

For is indicated by the F stem joined to the remainder of the word. The *accented* vowel *governs position*.

forsake	fortune	foresee
former	fortunate	foresight
forsaken	fortify	forehead
forsooth	forego	foremost
forgive	forethought	foreknown
forgot	forefather	foreground
forebode	foretaste	forewarn
foretell	foregone	foreclosure
	forejudge	

Magna, Magne, Magni.—By M stem written partly over the remainder of the word.

magnanimously	magnific
magnificence	magnetism

Self.—By a small circle *on* the line, and joined to following stem if it be a *down* stroke without circle or hook; otherwise, the following stem is written *close* to the *self* circle.

When *con* follows *self*, the dot must also be used.

self-abasement	self-dependence	self-convicted
self-assumed	self-protection	self-conceit
self-deceived	self-approving	self-condemn
self-determined	self-pleasing	self-conscious
self-destruction	self-important	self-complacent

With, by the word sign *dhr joined* to the remainder of the word, the *accented* vowel governing position.

withstand	within
withstood	withal
withheld	withdrawn
withhold	withdrawal

LESSON XVII.

Suffixes are indicated as follows:

Ble, Bly.—By B stem *joined* when hook is not easily shown.

    profitable   lamentable
    unattainable   unfashionable
    insensibly   defensible
    admissible   unpardonable
    unaccuntable   unwarrantable
    incontestable   reprehensible

Bleness, Fulness, Iveness, Lessness.—By Bs, Fs, Vs, Ls, *disjoined.*

BLENESS.

variableness   profitableness   acceptableness

FULNESS.

thoughtfulness   deceitfulness   faithfulness
wastefulness   gracefulness   hopefulness
hatefulness   cheerfulness   fruitfulness
fretfulness   doubtfulness   wakefulness
frightfulness   dolefulness   gratefulness

IVENESS

secretiveness   exclusiveness
massiveness   pursuasiveness

LESSNESS.

artlessness   guiltlessness   recklessness
groundlessness   needlessness   endlessness
blamelessness   matchlessness   shamelessness

Ever.—By the *v* hook, which may be added to *curved* stems.

    however   whichever   whoever
    whenever   whatever   wherever

SUPPLEMENTARY LESSONS.

Form.—By the F stem *joined.*

| deform | uniform |
| platform | informing |

Ing.—After *half-length* P or B, or when NG *stem* cannot be used, by a dot written at the end of the preceding part of the word.

Ings.—By a small circle written in the same manner.

putting	braiding	anticipating
beating	brooding	combating
biting	debating	nesting
petting	adopting	resting
abetting	adapting	investing
spotting	outbidding	coasting
spouting	debiting	festering
plating	reporting	·biddings
blotting	purporting	pleadings
bleeding	participating	buildings

Mental or *Mentality.*—By Mnt *disjoined.*

| ornamental | detrimental |

Ology.—By J stem *joined* or *disjoined* and written partly under.

meteorology	chronology
etymology	doxology
tautology	entomology
mineralogy	ichthyology

Self.—By small circle *joined.*
Selves.—By large circle *joined.*

yourself	herself	ourselves
himself	myself	themselves
itself	thyself	yourselves

Ship.—By the SH stem *joined* or *disjoined.*

worship	heirship	wardship
stewardship	guardianship	companionship
scholarship	copartnership	apprenticeship

Soever.—By sV *joined.*

    whensoever   whatsoever
    wheresoever   whichsoever

Worthy.—By the *DH joined* or *disjoined.*

    untrustworthy   unworthy   praiseworthy

CONSONANTS OMITTED.

The *t* sound after *s* circle in the *middle* of words.

lastly	dustpan	postponing
lasting	frosting	postpaid
restless	postmaster	boastful
testimonials	investigation	textbook
customers	domestics	mistaken
interesting	investments	requesting
testament	tastefully	custom house

N before Jr in the *middle* of words.

manager	lounger	plunger
ginger	messenger	ranger
passenger	infringer	harbinger

K omitted.

direction	respect
prospects	respective
directly	respectful
practical	extravagance

Final syllables, *ntial*, *ntially*.

    confidential-ly   prudential-ly
    financial-ly   providential-ly
            credential

N hook sometimes omitted in the *middle* of words.

atonement	transaction	transmission
attainment	transacting	translation
transfer	transmit	translucent
transact	transmutation	transportation

LESSON XVIII.

PHRASES.

Those formed by joining simple outlines or word signs, the *first* word to stand in its proper position.

In the middle or at the end of a phrase, *time* should be written with the T stem, and *that* should be made half-length.

may be	great while	any one
he was	for such	at hand
for that	does so	there was
will be	in answer	bill lading
it may	by this	in relation
shall be	on this	in accordance
should you	this day	very sorry
for which	this time	very glad
they were	in this	bills payable
so many	at this	bills receivable
if such	must be	some mistake
if he	no use	having been
that may	he must	must have
on them	at present	price list
so much	was taken	with reference
could do	young man	any person
for him	every side	in evidence
with me	dear sir	which one
that they	dear friend	any more
can be	there were	one thing
with him	we feel	very much
for any	short time	be sure
after each	only one	no one
for me	over charge	no more
under these	over which	should not be
no doubt	sight draft	it may be
on that	not been	by which means
so that	with regard	after many years
by which	assure you	many years ago
after all	in regard	to-morrow morning
that many	in reply	when he was
any time	in receipt	for my own

SUPPLEMENTARY LESSONS. 45

in any way	stock on hand	how many times
after several years	that will be	about that time
that they will	after that time	upon this point
on these points	for my sake	my dear friend
which must be	for some reason	my dear madam
we assure you	may be written	yours respectfully
for many years	after he was	sincerely yours
in your city	after he came	very sincerely yours
so many years	while he was	yours in haste
that he was	in this respect	yours very truly
so much so	that was said	that he has done
on my part	look at this	just about this time
cash on hand	in no wise	that they may be

Words should never be joined when there is a pause of any kind between them.

CIRCLES IN PHRASES.

The small circle for *as, has, is, his,* may be joined to any stem or word sign, both initially and finally.

It may be also used for *us* finally, but should never be joined to a verb.

The *first stem word* of the phrase must stand in the proper position.

as you	has part	thank his
is in	has our	come as
by his	change his	as have
how is	with his	over us
where is	as are	worth his
as much	has no	as they
beyond his	has all	with his
as may	when is	there is
from his	as at	as shall
so as	why is	as will
should his	as another	should his
that is	did his	as this
do as	charge us	as fast
by us	can his	such as
has her	has any	if he has
it is	as could	has not been

as you may	as good as	it is not
as we can	as she has	there is no
as we will	as many as	but has been
as could be	there is not	he has not been
as we think	it is necessary	it has been done
as bad as	there has been	as you may be
as young as	for such as	as far as may be

Doubling the size of the circle adds another circle word. The *first* word in the double circle governs position.

as has	has as	as his	is his
has his	as is	is as	his is

A circle word may be united to a word beginning or ending with a circle by doubling the size of the circle.

this is	this has been	as long as his
knows his	he has said	that this has been
miss his	as this is	as soon as possible
because his	it is his	as soon as this is
because his is	this city	as much as has been

To, it, the, may be added to a *circle* by changing it to a small loop. When joined to a stem, the stem must govern position; but when loop stands alone, the *circle* word governs. If more convenient, loop can be made first and stem added.

has to	because the	it is the	is it necessary
is it	because it	as to what	as it has to be
is the	as it was	has to be	as much as it
is to	as to these	as to this	has it not (1)
has the	has it been	as it ought	is it not (3)

There, their, they are, added by changing circle to *large* loop.

as they are	when is there
because there	is there any use
unless there	is there any one
since there	has there not been
has there been	has there not (1)
has there never	is there not (3)

Placing a circle inside large or small loop, adds another circle word to the phrase.

as to his	as there is
is to his	as there has
is it his	as they are his
as it has	as there has not (1)
as it is	as there is not (3)

LESSON XIX.

PHRASES WITH HOOKS.

All, will, added by the *l* hook.

in all
she will
we will
all will
at all
where all
when will
that all
or all

in all this
in all respects
she will be
we will be
we will believe
we will receive
it will be
in all my
what will you

Are, our, or, added by the *r* hook.

in our
from our
you are
where are
that are
these are
on or before

in our times
on our part
for our sake
at our suggestion
in our respect
on or about
in our letter

We to *straight* stems by the *w* hook.

did we
can we find
which we believe
what we say

can we believe
can we claim
had we been
could we believe

You, your, to *straight* stems by the *y* hook.

do you believe
which you say
what you recollect
had you been
did you receive

how do you
at your place
can you inform me
what did you say
what do you mean

In.—By the *in* curl.

in some other
in some way
in some degree
in some places

in some manner
in some cases
in some regards
in some respects

SUPPLEMENTARY LESSONS.

Have, of, added by the *f* hook.

think of	did have	side of	that they have
half of	may have	inside of	did you have
will have	should have	much of	what you have
each of	city of	copy of	each of these
what have	state of	both of	what have they
you have	number of	lack of	which of them
are of	receipt of	outside of	out of business
but have	subject of	which you have	out of town
know of	speak of	that you have	as long as they have

And, an, own, been, than, added by *n* hook.

for an	such an	having been	has your own
had been	easier than	their own	any more than
with an	longer than	stronger than	from our own
my own	larger than	had we been	between you and
our own	slower than	up and down	there must have been

There, their, they are, other, added by the *ter* hook or *lengthening.*

ought there	making their	in any other
where there	writing their	by all their
what other	winning their	at all other
could there	earning their	although they are
which other	remain there	some other cases
be there	came there	some other respects
did there	each of their	out of their
call their	can there be	may have their
but they are	here and there	care of their
should there	every other day	state of their
these other	among other things	in other words
every other	in other words	with the other
with other	any other time	although there is
where they are	the other day	that there has been
which they are	would have their	had you been there
at their	should have their	any part of their
between their	at other times	did you go there

SUPPLEMENTARY LESSONS.

The, it, had, to, added by halving.

in the	wish to	if it is
for the	able to	but it is
between the	unable to	though it is
before the	they had	why it is
upon the	have had	that it is
through the	she had	out of the
may the	it had	state of the
could the	part of the	outside of the
buy it	day of the	on the subject of
when it	which of the	may not have been
beyond it	charge of the	it may not be
was it	much of the	for the sake of the
near it	ought to be	at the present time
charge it	(above the	on the part of the
mean to	make the	at the same prices
began to	if he had	during the latter part of the

After.—By *f* hook and lengthening.

day after to-morrow	week after next
day after day	week after week

Another.—By *n* hook and lengthening.

if another	such another
though another	should another
shall another	in another way
why another	at another date

Its.—By halving and *s* circle.

with its	through its
should its	shall its
had its	by its

Not.—By *n* hook and halving.

cannot	shall not	they are not
could not	if not	you are not
was not	should not	would not be
have not	will not	it will not be
had not	would not	it could not be

A small hook may be turned inside of a large one.

had there been	rather than
but their own	at their own
any better than	by their own
greater than	as you have been
they have been	as we have been
may have been	at all their own
that have been	it may have been
much better than	that you have been
you have been	should never have been

Was, one. may be written with *w* hook, *n* hook and *s* circle.

what one	at one
which one	at once
each one	it was
had one	what was

SPECIAL SIGNS AND PHRASES.

............at length

............at all events

............at one time

............at the same time

............at any rate

............in the mean time

............some time

............heretofore

............we therefore

............had therefore

............he is therefore

............that therefore

............more or less

............day or two

SUPPLEMENTARY LESSONS.

.... said or done
.... faster than
.... less than
.... for instance
.... at last
.... at least
.... on the other hand
.... just as good as
.... meanwhile
.... State of New York
.... in the city of New York
.... typewriter
.... Sunday

.... Monday
.... Tuesday
.... Wednesday
.... Thursday
.... Friday
.... Saturday
.... one
.... six
.... one or two
.... one or more
.... two or three
.... two or more
.... three or four

SUPPLEMENTARY LESSONS.

..... cents

..... hundreds

..... thousands

..... millions

..... per cent

..... pro rata

..... et cetera

..... real estate

..... first class

..... in order

..... and so forth

..... January

..... February

..... March

..... April

..... May

..... June

..... July

..... August

..... September

..... October

..... November

..... December

..... Oh, yes

..... circular

..... circulars

LESSON XX.

TICKS.

I is a light tick struck like CH or Ree. When standing alone, it should be above the line. When joined to a stem, it never governs position. It should be struck upward before *can* and *could*.

I takes hooks as follows:

..⸱⸱⸱⸱⸱⸱ *I will*, with the tick struck upward.

..⸱⸱⸱⸱⸱⸱ *I have*, with the tick struck downward.

..⸱⸱⸱⸱⸱⸱ *I will not*, with the *n* hook added.

PHRASES WITH *I* TICKS.

I have	I hope	if I have any	
I will	I believe	if I may not	
I have not	I suppose	that I might	
I will not	I wish	that I shall be	
I thank	I remember	I am sorry	
I own	I fear	I am glad	
I was	I want	I said so	
I propose	I take	I have never	
I saw	or I	I may receive	
I show	may I	I thought that	
I come	shall I	I see this is	
I might	when I	I may as well	
I cannot	if I	I know there has been	
I am not	that I have	I would have been	
I had not	that I am	I think there is	
I did not	if I may	I think you have	
I understood	that I shall	I wish there was	
I could have	that I was	I suppose this is	
I may be	may I not	I have nothing	

SUPPLEMENTARY LESSONS.

When standing alone, *an* or *and* is indicated by a dot *above* the line; *a*, by dot *on* the line; *the*, a dot *below* the line.

A, an, and, may be joined to any word by a little tick struck *invariably* in the direction of P when used *initially:* but, in the middle or at the end of a phrase, it must be inclined to form the best angle.

The *n* hook should always be used, if possible, for *an* or *and*.

A, AN, AND TICKS.

a home	a great	round an	if a man
an age	under a	with a	in a short time
a law	have a	upon a	in a few days
a rule	save a	above a	for a month
and will	seen a	a great deal	before and after
and those	in a	a great many	and yet there has
and this	stay a	more than a	and that has been

The.—When halving or changing circle to small loop cannot be used, a perpendicular or horizontal tick may be added to indicate *the*. This should only be used finally.

THE TICK.

met the	spend the	ponder the
hit the	whether the	surrender the
need the	enter the	like the
hand the	order the	shoulder the

To, too, are indicated by a small *light* tick, *always* written *below* the line in the direction of P. It is used initially in phrasing, and governs position.

to me	to hand	to begin
to give	too many	to hate
to meet	to hide	to make
	to him	to mean

Who, Whom.—By a *heavily* shaded tick, *always below* the line, struck in the direction of J. This tick takes hooks like the J stem, and governs position of phrases.

SUPPLEMENTARY LESSONS.

who are	who was	who begin
who will	who could	who make
who have	who may	who minister
who will not	who give	who was not
who have not	who know	who may be

Of.—By a light tick like Ree, written above the line, and struck upward when alone, but up or down when joined.

The stem *of* is found to conflict seriously with *have;* therefore it is best to use the tick, and dispense entirely with both the stem and proximity for *of.*

of them	of our	of it	of their
of yours	of all	of its	of no use
of us	of hers	of such	of my own
of mine	of that	of worth	of your city
of many	of this	of course (1)	want of money
of other	of what	spoken of	point of view

We, would.—By the *w* brief sign.
You, your.—By the *y* brief sign.

FOLLOWING FORMS SHOULD BE MEMORIZED.

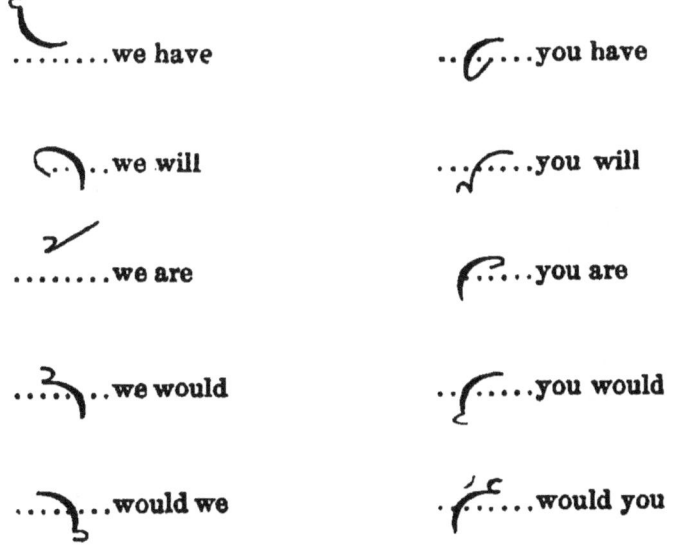

SUPPLEMENTARY LESSONS.

W BRIEF SIGNS.

we go
we could
we think
we are
we see
we fear
we beg
we found
we have
we know
we hope
we understand
we began
we remain
we inclose
we cannot
we regret
we wish
we request
we ought to
we did not
we had not
we shall be
we should have
we are sorry
we are sure
we should feel
we would beg
we would be
we could be
we shall have
we are not
we have yours
we could not
we think there is

we should have been
we ought to be
we have this day
would say
would think
would do
would be
would not be
if we
should we
they would
that we
but we
who would (*who* tick)
who would be (*who* tick)
who would not (*who* tick)
shall we be
shall we say
if we take
she would be
it would be
had we been
that would be
that we have
if you would
that we shall
that we had
when we shall
which we might
but we have
whether we be
which we now
what we can
it would have been
he would no doubt

Y BRIEF SIGNS.

you know	you ought to be	in your power
you made	you say you could	if you do
you cannot	your name	on your part
you recollect	your letter	in your case
you find	your entire	that you might
you intend	your orders	yet you make
you represent	your money	among all your
you may	from you	in all your
you must	inform you	that you will
you see	for you	what you can
you may not	with you	if you can
you should say	thank you	that you can
you could do	that you	that you are
you will find	in your	when you go
you will have	ask you	if you will
you must be	send you	that you may
you will not	pay you	if you are
you may be	informing you	if you cannot
you may have	which you	if you know
you must have	asking you	if you were there
you will have	when you	allow you on your
you will please	assuring you	that you will have
you will use	on your	so that you may
you do not know	if you	if you are not
you say you will	think you will	that you may be
you say you were	or you will	that you may have
you say you made	by your line	so that you make
you say there is	in your invoice	for which you were
you know there has	in your favor	do you mean to pay

When *com* or *con* follows *I* or *of,* the tick may take the place of the dot.

When *a, an, and,* or *the* follows a word for which the *ing* dot is required, either of these ticks may be used instead of the dot.

I commend	I confess	of common
I condemn	I contend	of committee
I complain	I command	of contract

SUPPLEMENTARY LESSONS.

adopting a	putting the	interesting the
arresting a	fostering the	ministering the
casting a	dating the	cheating the
testing the	doubting the	assisting the
bidding the		

When *to* is followed by a word the position of which is governed by a full or double length perpendicular or inclined stem, *to* may be omitted and shown by placing the outline *entirely* below the line. This is called the *fourth* position.

to be	to thank	to follow	to request
to have	to believe	to prove	to become
to do	to move	to receive	too early
to say	to keep	to live	to observe
to your	to place	to cover	to conduct
to this	to take	to look	to have been

LIST OF TICKS.

First position, ...*I* (up or down)   ......I will

  ......I have

  ......I will not

  ......I have not

Third position, ... *who, whom* (down)...... who are

  ...... who will

  ...... who are not

  ...... who will not

  ...... who have

  ...... who have not

First position, ... *of* (up when alone)

Third   "   ...... *to, too* (downward)

  ...... *a, an, and* (only used when joined)

  ...... *the* (only used when joined).

SUPPLEMENTARY LESSONS.   59

First position, ... *an, and* (when alone)

Second "   ..... *a* (when alone)

Third "   ..... *the* (when alone)

              ..... *we would* (always joined)

              ..... *you, your* (always joined)

First position, ... *awe* (alone)

Second "   ..... *owe, O, Oh* (alone)

TICKS, ETC., JOINED.

FIRST POSITION.   **THIRD POSITION.**

.... and I, a, an   .... to whom

.... and the   .... to a

.... and of   .... to the

.... of a   .... who would

.... of the   .... of whom

.... and as or his   .... to his

.... and as I, a

.. or .. as I

.... of his (upward)

TICKS, BRIEFS, CIRCLES AND LOOPS JOINED

to whom	of a	who has
and the	to the	to a
to his	who is	of as
of the	of whom	who have
who would	as I	who is
and a	and of	has not (1)

is not (3)	and is it	and is there (3)
and I	who are not	as I would
and as (1)	and as a (1)	and I will not
and is	and is a (3)	as I have not
of his	as I have	and as it is (1)
who would	and I have	and is it as (3)
and as I	and I will	and as there is
and I am	as to the (1)	and as to that
and as to (1)	is to the (3)	and as to the
and is the (3)	to whom we	and I have not
and has the	and as there (1)	and as there is not

PHRASES COMBINING ALL RULES.

and this	on the contrary	on the other hand
knows your	inasmuch	I am in receipt
wishing you	for some time	at the same time
to collect	to give you	you do not want
I have been	I have your	we have your favor
as a rule (1)	to meet you	I hope you can
as I am (*I* down)	we will have	I will not have
as I was (*I* down)	I will not say	and I am not
as I think (*I* up)	I do not understand	I have no other
as I know (*I* up)	I did not say	I cannot be there
we thank you	and yet there is	state of the case
have all been	I hope you will	on the part of the
that you have	I will be there	I will not pay
as we have	and that this is	and I have no doubt
as they have	I think there is	we have been there
that I am	we do not think	for I have not been
and you may	that we have been	I think you will be
we have had	to whom you refer	I think you have been
I am not	and though there is	as I have not yet
I shall have	if it is not	we think you will find
in all his	in a great many cases	I am in receipt of your
my own knowledge	I think you will	we have drawn on you
and my own	I have no doubt	yours truly
we give you	I have this day	yours respectfully
some time ago	in receipt of your	yours very respectfully
to call your	had he been there	I am yours sincerely
whom you could	at the present time	I am yours very truly

In writing amounts, the words million, thousand, hundred, dollars and cents should be written in shorthand; as,

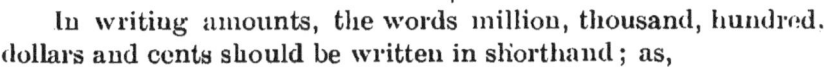

for $5,200,102.06.

Fractions with one for the numerator are written with the figure *one* very long, and denominator joined to it; as,

The line of writing may be used for fractional line in larger fractions.

In quoting range of prices, *to* is shown by placing the following figure entirely below the line (4th position); and *or*, by placing following figure above the line; as,

WORDS DISTINGUISHED.

cost caused			before above		
God guide			station situation		
train turn			valuation violation		
gentleman agent			count account		

SUPPLEMENTARY LESSONS.

appeal
bill......

honestly
nicely......

profit
provide......

marked
market......

finely
finally......

cancel
counsel......

character
caricature......

oppression
operation......

gradation
graduation......

level
lovely......

bread
board......

cramped
crammed......

beautiful
pitiful......

ingenious
ingenuous......

cordially
gradually......

birth
breath......

partner
part-owner......

prosecution
persecution......

protect
product......

protection
production......

appropriation
preparation......

extension
extenuation......

garden
guardian......

traitor
trader......

SUPPLEMENTARY LESSONS. 63

profaned
prevent

melt
mold

melter
molder

funeral.
funereal

oppressor
pursuer
peruser

month
minute
Monday

little
lately

detect
deduct

accepting
expecting

accepted
expected

writer
reader

advice
device

mission
machine

missionary
machinery

repression
reparation

interested
understood

undefined
indefinite

invasion.
innovation

nobody
anybody

violent
valient

indication
induction

debtor
editor

decease
disease

SUPPLEMENTARY LESSONS.

deceased
diseased..........

administration
demonstration..........

adoration
duration..........

poor
pure..........

purpose
propose..........

pattern
patron..........

property
propriety..........

corn
grain..........

bright
broad..........

staid
steady..........

favored
favor it..........

fierce
furious..........

proposal
proposition..........

Mrs.
Misses..........

latitude
altitude..........

island
land..........

erroneously
earnestly..........

fiscal
physical..........

weed
wood
wheat..........

hardly
heartily
hardly..........

sport
support
separate
spread..........

SENTENCES CONTAINING WORDS DISTINGUISHED.

I could not *prevent* their going away.
He was a very *profane* man.
They gave us very good *advice*.
It was quite an *ingenious device*.
The *character* of the man was *above* reproach.
It was a perfect *caricature* of herself.
There was a full *account* in the paper.
They will *count* the votes next *Monday*.
What is the *valuation* of that *property*?
That is a *violation* of a well known law.
The *cost* was more than the original *proposition*.
This *caused* his *partner* to change his plans.
I *understood* that they had *lately* built an *extension*.
There is nothing to say in *extenuation* of the evils of his *administration*.
The *indication* is that the *market* will *gradually* weaken, owing to the large *production* of *corn*.
Her manner is quite *ingenuous* and *lovely*.
There is a *steady* and *marked* advance in *wheat*.
The *oppression* of the *poor* in Russia is *pitiful*.
The *operation* was of shorter *duration* than was *expected*.
The *Board* of Foreign *Missions earnestly appeals* for aid.
The *profit* on *bread* making by *machinery* has been *erroneously* stated.
We are *cramped* for funds, as the *appropriation* was too small for the *purpose*.
Just *before graduation* the pupils are usually *crammed*.
I *cordially support* the *gentleman* for the *prosecution*.
An *island* is *land* surrounded by water.
He *finally* became a *missionary*, and was *valiant* for the cause.
The *situation* of the house is at an *altitude* of four thousand feet *above* the *level* of the sea.
Clay *molders* are numerous, and do some *beautiful* work.
He is *part-owner* of the *machine* which is in *preparation*.
The *gradation* you *propose* meets my approval.
I am *heartily interested* in the *protection* of the *writer* of the *little* book, now in the hands of the *editor*, called "*Physical Culture*."

Phonography seems to be the *favorite* study.
Mrs. Smith was *finely* dressed, having a long *train*.
Nobody favored the *fierce prosecution* of the *debtor*.
The *wood spread* across the *broad* valley.
I *hardly expected* they would *deduct* from the *bill* after *accepting* the *pattern*.
Why did you make such *sport* of your *staid guardian?*
At last they had to *separate* at the *station*.
He was a *bright* child, but he held his *breath* when he cried.
His *birth* place was in the Southern *latitude*.
The *broad* avenues of our capital are *beautiful*.
He was a *traitor* to his country, and was soon caught by his *pursuer*.
The *deceased* man left no will. His *disease* was consumption. He was a *trader* in the West.
Violent acts and *furious demonstrations* are uncalled for in meeting the *oppressor*.
May the *God* of our fathers be your *guide*.
It is pleasant to *breathe* the *pure* air in the *garden* in the *month* of May.
We will consider the *propriety* of *accepting* your *proposal*.
Anybody may be a *peruser* of the papers for *at least* a few *minutes* every day.
The *funeral* of the *deceased* took place last *Monday*.
The *product* of our land is entirely *grain*—mostly *wheat* and some *corn*.
We must *protect* our *agent*, and make the *reparation* he demands.
The *repression* of the rebellion was accomplished after many *invasions*.
Expecting he would *detect* the error and *honestly correct* the *account*, we did not employ *counsel*.
It was quite an *innovation*, and seemed to *provide* the *Misses* D—— with much amusement.
Write your outlines as *nicely* and accurately as possible.
The *fiscal* year is now near its close.
The *demonstration* was one of *pure adoration*, but one of short *duration*.
The *gentleman* is an *agent*, not a *partner* in the business.
They must *melt* the iron *before* they can *turn* it into the *mold*.

Your statement is very *indefinite*.
His *induction* into office occurred last week.
He was one of my first *patrons*.
"Man *proposes*, but God *disposes*."
"By *induction* Franklin established the identity of lightning and electricity; by *deduction* he inferred that dwellings might be *protected* by lightning rods."

LAW WORDS AND PHRASES.

above........	appertaining........
adjudicate.....	appurtenances......
administrators..	arraignment......
administratrix.	assigns........
administration.	attorney-at-law........
advice.....	at and before....
advised.....	at or before......
affidavit....	counsel........
aforesaid....	codicils......
appellant......	complainants.....

SUPPLEMENTARY LESSONS.

constitute.......

corporator..........

counter complaint........

covenants..........

cross-examine........

cross-examination........

recross-examination........

day and year........

debenture........

decedent........

defendant........

defendant's counsel........

demurrer........

deponent........

deposes........

deposition........

devised........

devisee........

direct examination........

redirect examination........

ensealing........

executors........

executrix........

foresee........

foregoing........

forever........

SUPPLEMENTARY LESSONS.

grantor..................

grantee..................

hereat...................

hereby..................

hereditaments..........

herein...................

hereinafter.............

hereinbefore...........

hereinunder............

hereon..................

hereto...................

heretofore..............

hereof..................

hereunto................

herewith................

heir-at-law.............

howsoever..............

immaterial..............

indenture...............

injunction...............

in testimony whereof......

In witness whereof, I have hereunto set my hand and seal......

irrelevant................

judicature...............

judgment................

SUPPLEMENTARY LESSONS.

jurisdiction

jurisprudence

know all men by these presents

last will and testament

lawful-ly

legatee

mortgage

mortgagee

mortgagor

notarial

object

objected to

objection sustained

on or about

or otherwise

otherwise

objection overruled

objected to as immaterial

party of the first part

party of the second part

patent

patentee

personal estate

plaintiff

SUPPLEMENTARY LESSONS. 71

plaintiff's counsel..........

power of attorney........

referee................

relator................

respondent................

released ....

relevant................

reversion..............

shall and will..............

signed, sealed and delivered in the presence of..........

special term..............

specifications............

state of the case..........

supervisory..............

superior court............

supreme court............

testator................

testimony..............

testamentary............

thereafter..............

thereat................

therefor-e..............

therein................

thereof................

thereon................

SUPPLEMENTARY LESSONS.

thereto	wheresoever
thereunto	whereat
thereupon	wherefore
therewith	wherein
to wit	whereof
to have been	whereon
to hold	whereto
waive	whereupon
warrant	wherever
we therefore	wherewith
whatever	whomsoever
whatsoever	witness
whensoever	witnesseth

SUPPLEMENTARY LESSONS.
WORD SIGNS AND CONTRACTIONS.

A

	Bankruptcy	Catholic
According	Baptism	Celestial-ly
Acknowledge	Because	Certificate
Advantage	Become	Change
Advertise	Before	Characteristic
Almost	Began	Charge
Already	Begin	Children
Altogether	Begun	Christian
Among	Belief-ve	Circumstance
Angel	Belong	Circumstantial
Another	Benignant	Citizen
Antagonistic	Between	Collect
Any	Beyond	Come
Archangel	Bishopric	Controversy
Archbishop	Brethren	Correct
Architecture-al	Brother	Could
Are	But	County
Aristocracy-tic		Cross-examine
Artificial	Cabinet	
Astonish-ed	Can	December
	Capable	Defendant
Bankrupt	Captain	Degree

B

C

D

SUPPLEMENTARY LESSONS.

Deliver........................Endeavor....................Gentlemen.................
Democracy-tic................Especial-ly..................Give-n......................
Democrat.....................Establish....................Go..........................
Describe......................Evangelical.................Govern.....................
Description..................Ever.........................Governor..................
Develop......................Executrix...................Great Britain..............
Did...........................Experience.................
Differ-ence-ent..............Extraordinary..............
Difficult-y....................   **H**
                             F   Had.........................
Dignify.......................Fact.........................Half........................
Dignity......................Familiar....................Halve......................
Discriminate.................Familiarity.................Hath.......................
Distinct......................February...................Have.......................
Distinguish..................Financial-ly................He.........................
Do...........................First........................Health-y..................
Dr. (Doctor).................For.........................Hear.......................
Doctrine.....................Form.......................Heaven....................
Dollar........................Frequent...................Help........................
Domestic....................From.......................Her........................
During.......................   Here.......................
Dwell........................Gave.......................Him........................
                             E
                             General-ly..................History....................
Effect........................Gentleman.................Home......................

SUPPLEMENTARY LESSONS.

I

Immediate
Importance-t
Inartificial-ly
Indignity
Indispensable-y
Influence
Influential
Inscribe
Insurance
Intelligence
Intelligent
Interrogatory

J

January
Jr. (Junior)
Jurisprudence

K

Kingdom
Knew
Knowledge

L

Language

Large
Legislature
Length-y
Long (adj.)

M

Malignant
Manufactory
Manufacture
Manufacturer
Massachusetts
Member
Memoranda
Memorandum
Mistake
Mr. (Mister)
Mistook
Movement

N

Neglect
Never
Nevertheless
New
New York

Next
Notwithstanding
November
Now
Number

O

Ob'-ject
Object'
Objection
Observation
Oh
Opinion
Opportunity
Other
Our
Over
Own

P

Parliament
Part
Particular
Peculiar
Peculiarity

SUPPLEMENTARY LESSONS.

Pecuniary	Probability	Republic-sh
People	Probable-y	Repugnant
Performs	Proportion	Responsibility
Performance	Public-sh	Responsible-y
Perpendicular	**Q**	Resurrection
Perpendicularity	Quality	Rev. (Reverend)
Philanthropy	Quarter	Revolutionary
Philanthropic	Question	Roman Catholic
Phonographer	**R**	**S**
Phonographic	Recollect	San Francisco
Phonography	Recollection	Satisfaction
Plaintiff	Recoverable	Satisfactory
Plenipotentiary	Refer-ence	Savior
Popular-ity	Regular	September
Possible-y	Regularity	Several
Practicable-y	Religion	Shall
Practical-ly	Relinquish	Should
Practice	Reluctantly	Signify
Preliminary	Remark	Similar
Prerogative	Remember	Similarity
Preservation	Remembrance	Singular
Principal-le	Represent-ative	Somewhat
Privilege	Representation	Southern

SUPPLEMENTARY LESSONS.

Speak...... Them.... When....
Special-ly..... These ..... Where....
Spoke..... Thing..... Which.....
Subject..... Think..... Whom.....
Subjection..... Time..... Will.....
Suggestion..... Together..... With.....
Superficial-ly..... Transubstantiation..... Without.....
Superintendent..... Truth..... World.....
Surprise..... U Worth.....
Swear..... Understood..... Would.....
Swift..... Usual..... Y
Swore..... United States..... Year.....
Sympathy..... W Yet.....
System..... Was..... Young.....
Wealth-y..... Your.....
Thank-ed..... Well..... Youth.....
That..... Were.....
Their, There..... What.....

AN INCONSEQUENT HISTORY OF INCONGRUOUS THINGS.

No. 1.

An intelligent young man, having become antagonistic because a citizen would cross-examine him, together with his domestic, as to their religion, spoke to an archbishop who was familiar with his history, and asked him to take charge of the controversy. The Roman Catholic gentleman was astonished at the suggestion, but thanked the youth for the opportunity it gave him to develop his doctrine and help his generation. His brethren, nevertheless, were of the opinion that he should discriminate somewhat, and gave him the privilege to acknowledge his responsibility and establish his belief. Another circumstance should be understood as possibly distinguishing between prerogative and principle: the youth mistook the movement for a financial performance, and began to practice his malignant familiarity, which was a new thing in the experience of the evangelical brother, who swore somewhat, but yet did not go beyond the dignity of his Catholic and Christian endeavor.

This, it is well to remember, was in New York, before the first of January, when the Doctor was preaching transubstantiation, a truth not generally held, and the Governor of Massachusetts, a plenipotentiary from San Francisco, a member of Parliament from Great Britain, and other representative people were particular as to the perpendicularity of their belief. An angel from heaven could have had no difficulty to establish intelligence on the subject of insurance; and even the archangels who dwell on the resurrection, have found their knowledge altogether without importance in the peculiar contingency. The fact is, a Southern gentleman, to whom the question was given, began to make memoranda with reference to jurisprudence in the celestial world, and to inscribe in phonographic characteristics his own recollections and observations, and to speak of the objections and advantages of a Republic. A swift phonographer, with a memorandum-book, had part in the controversy, and several other capable gentlemen, among them a manufacturer, who was their captain, and a Democrat, began to remark on the effects of an aristocracy. The County Democracy, who are responsible for much neglect and misdemeanor, and who during, February, September, November, and December of each year manufacture revolutionary language for the Legislature, gave a satisfactory description of the difference between the plaintiff and defendant; and the Rev. Mr. Brown, ever ready to deliver his opinion, or to change it on any subject for a dollar, said, notwithstanding his surprise at the indignity shown him, he would never again have sympathy for a system without a pecuniary object.

I remember a time, now past, when preliminary bankruptcy

SUPPLEMENTARY LESSONS. 79

was healthy, and would influence people to swear; but do not infer from this that any bankrupt would think it practicable to do so. According to our distinct remembrance the architectural bishopric was circumstantial and artificial, and no certificate of baptism could dignify the mistake, or qualify the probability to the satisfaction of the junior member. The peculiarity of the half length in phonography is singular, but practical, and its preservation, because indispensable, will probably continue as usual, notwithstanding the number of perpendicular strokes out of proportion. These do not signify where similar strokes come together in a regular way. Regularity is what we owe to system. Wealth lies in that quarter, and worth. Your benignant people belong to this class, and to them we shall send a Saviour. Superficially. Truth hath her home here, and has had. oh ! so long. The immediate kingdom, though large, is no mere manufactory, as I recollect it. It is also recoverable in a degree by the public, and never overcrowded. Next to being under subjection to an executrix or an administratrix, it is repugnant to have a representation in the Cabinet, especially if one can govern himself, or advertise what is already begun or almost to begin. As this is altogether beneficial, I need not describe it nor mention it for children to hear with awe; but simply collect the facts and correct the errors, and thus halve the difficulties inartificially and in due form. To this regularity no one could specially object, because the frequent and peculiar evidences of popularity attending a similarity of movement everybody knew.

Financially speaking, the general condition of the Democratic party is not important; nevertheless, people differ according to their different temperaments, and it should not astonish any one that the wealthy give special care to health, and believe in avoiding superficial remedies, even though popular. The principal architecture of our large cities has especial reference to aristocratic taste, although it is inartificial and practically useless. But a lengthy dissertation is not possible, so this shall not be long. It will probably represent the celestially inclined, and refer to an interrogatory or two indispensably connected with the subject. Thank nobody for this, nor publish the fact, however responsibly it may be stated. This will not do to republish, for, oh ! it is so flat.

No. 2.

Mr Cleveland, Governor of New York, a gentleman of large experience, should know how to determine the peculiar principle of his own particular party, as he has had an advantage in connection with gentlemen of somewhat similar intelligence, who propose to do well, and will not do anything to their disadvantage; but, according to a memorandum which they made among themselves, before January, that is, between September and December, we think these important, influential, practical, and responsible persons can establish a government over the United States from Maine to San Francisco, whose significance you will here with truthfulness acknowledge, notwithstanding your counsel is different, and as member of another party, you have another object, other memoranda, and represent a company that, at the regular time this year, did all they were capable of doing to deliver the public property from danger.

Our opinion on this subject we owe to no man; nevertheless, as defendant, we shall swear that the plaintiff is not now indispensable, and we shall never remark that his influence is a thing of significant importance, where they are, in all probability, those who, like a new doctor, ever advertise for profit when any particular knowledge about the children or family will connect the fact, in a general yet circumstantial way, with what I could call irregular, in the frequent difficulty to exchange a dollar during bankruptcy, behind which I knew those familiar with insurance and manufacture to go.

Oh! I recollect a circumstance, difficult to explain in language without phonography. When Mr. Cleveland was pretty well up in the world, he thought it was practicable, I remember, to refer the opportunity of the hour during his principal performance to the quantity of truthful friends who, it was probable, would immediately perform their part with subjection upon his return home.

COMMON ERRORS IN SPELLING.

Final e is dropped before a suffix beginning with a vowel:

bite	bit-ing	desire	desir-ing
cure	cur-ing	compose	compos-ing
save	sav-ing	arrive	arriv-ing
sale	sal-able	receive	receiv-ing
give	giv-ing	balance	balanc-ing

Except in words ending in *ce* or *ge* when the suffix begins with *a* or *o;* or when final *e* is required to preserve the identity of the word.

pea*ce*-*a*ble	exchan*ge*-*a*ble	sin*ge*-ing
chan*ge*-*a*ble	mana*ge*-*a*ble	d*ye*-ing
noti*ce*-*a*ble	outra*ge*-*o*us	tin*ge*-ing
servi*ce*-*a*ble	coura*ge*-*o*us	ho*e*-ing
char*ge*-*a*ble	advanta*ge*-*o*us	sho*e*-ing

Although contrary to rule, custom sanctions dropping the final *e* in

abridgment
acknowledgment
lodgment
judgment

DOUBLING FINAL CONSONANT.

Words of one syllable, and those accented on the *last* syllable ending in a single consonant preceded by a single vowel, double the final consonant before a suffix *beginning* with a vowel:

beg	be*gg*ing	permit	permi*tt*ed
dip	di*pp*ed	infer	infe*rr*ed
begin	begi*nn*ing	occur	occu*rr*ence
prefer	prefe*rr*ed	sin	si*nn*er
control	contro*ll*able	rid	rid-*d*ance

Therefore and Therefor.— If *hence* can be substituted, use the word *therefore*. If *instead of*, then the word *therefor*.
Principal means *chief*, and must only be used in that sense.
Principle, original cause, a motive.
The word *capitol* is only used for a building.
Council, an assemby.
Counsel, advice, direction.
Consul, one appointed by the government to care for its commercial interests.

USE OF Z, C, S.

realize	advice (noun)
recognize	advise (verb)
authorize	device (noun)
civilize	devise (verb)
patronize	defense
apologize	expense
neutralize	offense
practice, or *se*	pretense

SIMPLE RULES FOR *EI* AND *IE*.

Ei follows *c* soft; as, *receive*; *ie* follows other consonants. Or, *i* before *e*, unless following *c*.

perceive	believe
receipt	relieve
deceive	reprieve
conceive	retrievable

APOSTROPHE.

Plural nouns which are formed by adding *s*, require only the apostrophe to denote possession. Plural nouns which are *not* formed by adding *s*, must have both apostrophe and *s*, the same as nouns in the singular number.

Girls' hats.	Burns's Poems.
Boys' coats.	An hour's work.
Ladies' calls.	Three years' lease.
Children's toys.	A dollar's worth.
Men's clothing.	

ABBREVIATIONS.

ad lib.	ad libitum (at pleasure)
con.	contra (against)
do.	ditto (the same)
e. g.	exempli gratiâ
et al.	et alibi — and elsewhere / et alii or aliæ — and others
etc., &c.	et cætera — and others / and so forth
et seq.	et sequentes (and the following)
ib.	ibidem (in the same place)
id.	idem (the same)
i. e.	id est (that is)
i. q.	idem quod (the same as)
pro tem.	pro tempore (for the time being)
SS. or ss.	scilicet (namely)
viz.	videlicet (namely)
Vs. or vs.	versus (against)

www.ingramcontent.com/pod-product-compliance
Lightning Source LLC
Chambersburg PA
CBHW031606110426
42742CB00037B/1305